W9-BZA-658

Gospel

The Life,
Times,
& Music
Series

Gospel

The Life, Times, & Music Series

o

Peter O. E. Bekker, Jr.

CONSULTING EDITOR FOR THE
LIFE, TIMES, & MUSIC SERIES:
PETER O.E. BEKKER, JR.

Friedman / Fairfax Publishers

A FRIEDMAN GROUP BOOK

©1993 by Michael Friedman Publishing Group, Inc.

All rights reserved. No part of this publication may be
reproduced, stored in a retrieval system, or transmitted, in any form
or by any means, electronic, mechanical, photocopying, recording,
or otherwise, without prior written permission from the publisher.

ISBN 1-56799-041-X

THE LIFE, TIMES, & MUSIC SERIES: GOSPEL
was prepared and produced by the
Michael Friedman Publishing Group, Inc
15 West 26th Street
New York, New York 10010

Editor: Nathaniel Marunas
Art Director: Jeff Batzli
Designer: Kingsley Parker
Photography Editor: Jennifer Crowe McMichael
Consulting Editor: Peter O.E. Bekker, Jr.

Grateful acknowledgment is given to authors, publishers,
and photographers for permission to reprint material. Every effort has
been made to determine copyright owners of photographs and
illustrations. In the case of any omissions, the publishers will be
pleased to make suitable acknowledgments in future editions.

Printed in the United States of America

For bulk purchases and special sales, please contact:
Friedman/Fairfax Publishers
15 West 26th Street
New York, NY 10010
(212) 685–6610 FAX (212) 685–1307

Acknowledgments

There was much to discover at the New York City Public Library's Schomburg Center for Research in Black Culture and Lincoln Center Branch. The author is grateful for the insights of Mrs. Thomas Dorsey and the help provided by the staff at Fisk University in Nashville and the Tindley Temple in Philadelphia. Thanks also to Nathaniel Marunas at the Michael Friedman Publishing Group for advancing the scope of this book into the present day.

Contents

Mahalia Jackson rose from humble beginnings in New Orleans to achieve international fame as the "Queen of Gospel."

Introduction

I n the history of music, gospel is not old. It arose on the

heels of the Pentecostal revivalism that swept the na-

tion at the turn of the twentieth century, blooming at

about the same time and in many of the same places

as its cousins, jazz and the blues. Like these cousins,

gospel is the creation of black Americans who fled the

rural South for northern cities after the Civil War,

bringing to their not entirely hospitable new homes the

folkways and traditional song forms—such as work

songs and congregational spirituals—that had sus-

tained them through centuries of slavery.

"Gospel" describes an emotional, devotional, spiri-

tual way of singing as well as a living body of work, a

repertoire that continues to grow and expand as new gospel songs are written, circulated, and sung. Gospel may be relatively new as a recognizable, definable musical form, but its roots are in the ancient cultures of Africa. More recently, gospel can be heard as the foundation of a great deal of today's pop music.

Two of the most widely recorded giants of the contemporary gospel scene, the Reverend James Cleveland (left) and Al Green, at Cleveland's Cornerstone International Church in the late 1970s, at a time when Green was electrifying audiences with both soul and gospel performances.

Gospel is generally written and performed as sacred music, usually in praise of the Christian God, but the style has also been secularized by such singers as Ray Charles (1930–), Aretha Franklin (1942–), Sam Cooke (1931–1964), B.B. King (1925–), Dinah Washington (1924–1963), Wilson Pickett (1941–), and Al Green (1947–). Their extrapolation of the form is called soul, which is often indistinguishable from gospel—except in its lyrics. Aretha Franklin's experience is common among soul singers: a daughter of the Reverend C.L. Franklin (1915–1984), a dynamic Baptist preacher and civil rights activist, Aretha first appeared publicly while she was still a girl, singing gospel songs in her father's Detroit church and performing in his evangelical road show. When she began making records for the Chess label in 1956, Aretha's focus gradually shifted to commercial, Top 40 songs that she delivered in an unmistakable gospel style. Even so, Aretha went on to become the "Queen of Soul," not the "Queen of Gospel," because she crossed the vivid line between the sacred and the secular that exists in the hearts and minds of gospel's purists similar to the line that separates the "saved" and the "unsaved." Once that line has been crossed, there is no

Above: Aretha Franklin's career as a soul singer was building when this photo was taken in 1962. Inset: The daughter of a prominent Baptist minister, Aretha sang gospel music during her girlhood and teenage years in her father's Detroit church and at revivals on the "gospel highway." In later years, she returned to gospel.

easy way back. Soul singers may dabble in gospel, and even sing songs in the gospel style, but only those who sing in praise of God are considered "true believers."

Africa

There is a certain irony in that purist outlook, which was held even more fervently in the early days of gospel than it is today. The music created by gospel's founders and early evangelists was fundamentally influenced by the folk music and spirituals of African-American slaves, a music that spoke more of the travails of life, oppression, bondage, and a longing for freedom than of redemption by God. Africans were not Christians when they endured the hard passage to the Americas, nor did they embrace Christianity in great numbers until quite late in the tragic, long-lived run of the slave trade.

Slaves and their tribal African forebears did not draw the distinction between sacred and secular music that is drawn today. For West Africans, music, song, and dance were used to observe and commemorate important events. Music and song accompanied nearly every tribal occurrence from births to deaths, hunts to feasts, and sowing to harvest—there were even songs in some tribes to commemorate so mundane an event as a child's first loss of a tooth. Since most African tribes had no tradition of written history, it was through songs, stories, and dances that important his-

In the South during the post–Civil War period, cotton pickers like these toiled inhumanly long, hard hours—with little reward—to make the white man rich. Spirituals and work songs were a source of inner strength for an oppressed people who had little control over their own outward existence.

In many African cultures, ritual meetings, ceremonies, songs, and dances were vital conduits for the transmission of tribal customs, lore, and folkways from generation to generation.

torical and cultural information moved from one generation to the next. Singers and storytellers were living encyclopedias of their people's culture. A tradition of rich oral history developed in which generation after generation learned the history, lore, and folkways of their people through active participation.

Secret Meetings

These folkways came to the Americas with enslaved Africans and were influenced and transformed over hundreds of years of bondage and oppression. Tribal songs were often used as a "secret language" with which slaves would, among other things, plot rebellions and escapes. The African tribal ritual of "secret meetings" (called Brush Arbor or Camp Meetings in the colonies), during which songs and lore were created, taught, and passed along, was also a fixture of slave life. Slaves would gather together in such meetings, often summoned to them, as their African ancestors had been, by the beat of a drum or the blowing of a horn. These meetings provided a sense of community and continuity to a people completely adrift in foreign surroundings, existing there in servitude. At the secret meetings, which were strictly segregated by sex and almost always held in the woods or at some other remote location unknown to the masters, slaves would take part in dances and song rituals that were sometimes frenzied and often lasted many hours. It was not uncommon for the participants to rage against their bondage and plan ways of escape, usually with Africa as the hoped-for destination. Nor was it unusual for the "minutes" of these meetings to emerge as a communal song.

Slave owners had good reason to fear rebellions, for there had been revolts in Haiti, Central America, and Venezuela that had been bloody conflicts. In order to prevent similar insurrections, colonies in North America, starting with Virginia in 1676, outlawed assemblies of African Americans and other "African cult" gatherings, specifically mentioning those that were called by the beat of a drum. There was no effective way, however, for slave owners to silence the collective voice of an enslaved people who steadfastly continued to express themselves about oppression and the dire circumstances of their lives, and to voice their determination to escape the chains of servitude.

This depiction of a Camp (or Brush Arbor) Meeting shows the frenzied pitch that such gatherings often reached. The locations of Camp Meetings, which often lasted through the night, were kept secret from slave owners.

Even the most common aspects of daily life, such as sowing crops, were celebrated in song, dance, or other rituals by West Africans and their enslaved brethren in the Americas.

Slave Songs and Spirituals

In North America this expression often took the form of chants and songs in the clipped and imprecise words of people who were new to the English language. As they had in Africa, these songs sometimes described everyday events such as waking, sleeping, working, playing, sowing, planting, harvesting, or worshiping. Other songs, however, with words either created extemporaneously or learned from Protestant hymns, and often embellished with "moaning" bluesy vocalizations, poignantly expressed the rage, pain, and hopelessness of enslavement. These were the chants and songs that have come to be known as spirituals.

The words of slave songs might have seemed harmless and simply pious, but in many cases those words concealed deeply buried meanings. There is evidence that Nat Turner (1800–1831), the

Nat Turner lobbied among the other slaves in Southampton County, Virginia, urging them to join his bloody 1831 revolt, which claimed seventy-three lives.

leader of a bloody slave revolt in Southampton County, Virginia, may have written the spiritual "Steal Away."

> Steal away, steal away,
> Steal away to Jesus,
> Steal away, steal away home,
> I ain't got long to stay here.

The song's authorship is uncertain, but it is known that Turner used the song to convene the meetings at which his rebellion was planned. In that light, the words might be interpreted like this: Steal away, steal away (come to a meeting); Steal away to Jesus (a chance for freedom); Steal away, steal away home (a chance to return to Africa); I ain't got long to stay here (slavery will soon be over, or, perhaps, our meeting must be short, because it is illegal).

Turner's rebellion, which took place in 1831, was brief, lasting only several days. Sixteen conspirators were either killed during the insurrection or hanged—like Turner himself. Before the rebellion was put down, Turner and his crew killed fifty-seven whites, an unlikely event to be heralded by a clarion call of such apparent piety as "Steal Away."

Biblical references abound in spirituals, but, as in "Steal Away," references of this kind in antebellum songs were mostly metaphorical. Christianity was not widespread among slaves, and biblical references in spirituals generally signified something else.

Christian slaves and free blacks held prayer meetings in their own, often makeshift, houses of worship. Many of the mainstream Christian denominations, particularly those in the South, did not allow blacks inside their churches.

White Gospel

As the term is used today, "gospel" is fundamentally a black music. Its rhythms, its soul, and its musical sensibilities spring from African roots and traditions that were transformed by centuries of slavery in the Americas. Its practice is the organic, sometimes unrestrained expression of that experience in exuberant Christian worship.

The earliest "black gospel" songs, circa 1850, were based mostly on psalms and hymns from the "white gospel"—the vast library of British Protestant hymnals and songbooks. These were the sacred songs written over the centuries by such composers as Isaac Watts, William Howard Doane (1831–1915), William B. Bradbury (1815–1868), and countless others. By the turn of the twentieth century, black preachers and black composers were writing both the words and the music in a budding repertoire that would finally evolve into the unique and far more flamboyant sacred style known as gospel music. Even though Catholic and Protestant hymnody are still widely practiced and haven't changed much over the years, it is likely that the emergence of black gospel was a prime force behind the recent development of another kind

of white gospel, the so-called "Christian music" that is sung to the beat of a pop band by performers such as Amy Grant.

The core difference between black and white gospel is certainly cultural. While black gospel has roots in the primal, spontaneous, supremely emotional expression of enslaved Africans—the keening and moaning songs of slaves, work songs, and spirituals—white gospel is based on the constrained, disciplined, pious, and humble worship practiced by European Protestants.

The shape-note singing of New England Puritans is a good example of the different approach to religious singing by the two cultures. The idea behind shape note, which was developed in the early 1700s, was to improve the quality of church singing and to provide visual clues that would identify words to people who could not read. It was a sing-by-numbers strategy, but instead of numbers or regular musical notes, the tones to be sung were represented by unique shapes such as diamonds, circles, and squares. This made it easy for anyone who understood the shape-note code to convincingly sing straightforward hymns. Because of the precision involved in singing one spe-

"White gospel" is still sung in a pious, decorous, unexuberant way—as much the result of cultural inclination as Puritan tradition.

Worship in black churches is very often spirited and emotionally charged. Music and uninhibited singing is an organic ingredient of prayer meetings (above) and weddings (below).

cific tone at a time, shape-note singing had a very distinctive and pleasing sound, but in practice it was impersonal, rote, and as far from spontaneous as it was possible to be. Shape-note singing became very popular and spread throughout the colonies and territories of North America, even into the South, where in the early 1800s Ananias Davisson (1780–1857) put together a songbook called *Sacred Harp*, a name by which shape-note singing is also known today.

The differences in approach are clear: white gospel is descended from traditions that are restrained and, in essence, learned from books; black gospel is descended from unrestrained, spontaneous emotion. That distinction still applies today, and because the two idioms are based in cultures that are diverse, will probably always apply. While the devotional purpose of each kind of gospel singing is more or less the same, the way in which Johnny Cash, Jimmy Dean, or Roy Acuff sings a gospel song will always differ dramatically from the way in which Sister Myrtle Fields, Sister Clara Hudmon, Marion Williams, or Mahalia Jackson sings one.

"Canaan," "heaven," and other references to the "Promised Land" were often metaphors for Africa or some other place of freedom. "Lord," "Jesus," "God," "Moses," "Mary," and other references to biblical figures usually signified a person of prominence in the particular place and time the spiritual was created. This might have been a clergyman, a teacher, or even a prominent slave respected for his or her wisdom. Even as Nat Turner was lobbying for his rebellion in the 1820s, Christianity was only just being spread and truly embraced in the slave quarters of the agrarian South.

In Mississippi Plantation, *Currier and Ives show plantation life as prim and orderly. The truth of the antebellum South, at least for blacks, was a far grimmer picture of slavery and desperate hopelessness in a near-feudal society.*

One reason for the introduction of religion among slaves was the white hope that the anger and unrest of the enslaved would be mellowed by Christian doctrine. Granted that the abiding view of slave owners was that Africans were soulless "black cattle," it is likely that the early goal of missionary work among slaves was to pacify them rather than to save their souls.

During the so-called Great Awakening, a religious revival that swept the American colonies between 1720 and 1750, a Presbyterian minister in Virginia named Samuel Davies (1723–1761) distributed

religious songbooks to slaves. In the mid-1700s he wrote of his apprehensions about the growing militancy of African Americans, a development he found particularly dangerous because Native Americans and the French were already making matters difficult by invading colonial settlements at that time. From his ministry in Hanover, Virginia, Davies contacted the London Society for Promoting Christian Knowledge, which sent him copies of *Watts Psalms and Hymns and Bibles*, the work of Isaac Watts (1674–1748), pastor of the independent Mark Lane congregation in London and composer of a considerable number of hymns. (Watts' hymns became so familiar to slaves that the term "Dr. Watts" was often used to describe any hymn, whether or not it was composed by Watts.) In a letter of thanks, Davies asked for more of the volumes, profusely describing the joy with which slaves had embraced the books and the songs they contained.

Reverend Isaac Watts, the British cleric whose many religious songs remain staples of Protestant hymnody.

The dynamic black preacher, seen here in front of a captivated congregation, was a popular and ubiquitous image.

At the end of the nineteenth century, freed slaves embarked on a massive migration from the Reconstructionist South to northern U.S. cities.

From 1795 through the 1840s, another wave of religious revivalism, known as the Second Great Awakening, swept the then-fledgling nation. While its precursor had been based in Calvinist theology, which viewed God as the only arbiter of the soul, the Second Awakening was driven by Arminianism, which allowed for human decisions in the process of salvation—in other words, people could decide for themselves whether to embrace God. It also taught that every living thing was eligible to be saved. In many denominations, this included slaves.

The end of the Civil War wrought monumental changes in the lives of the ruling class in the feudal South, but only briefly and haltingly did it change the lives of blacks. African Americans benefited from the social adjustments that accompanied the South's defeat, but really only during the earliest days of Reconstruction. While emancipation from slavery was at the top of the list of improvements, blacks also became eligible for schooling and were allowed to attend free public schools. In addition, Southern states eliminated racially discriminatory laws, and some of the states even outlawed racial discrimination by individuals. But the promise of the early post–Civil War years was ultimately to prove a dream deferred for the thousands of former slaves. Windows of opportunities, never fully opened for them, were slammed shut almost immediately with the onset of Jim Crow laws in the late 1800s. These laws, named after a mocking minstrel show caricature, fostered and justified a "separate but equal" caste system in most Southern states, sanctioned by the 1896 U.S. Supreme Court ruling in the case of Plessy v. Ferguson. It was during this period of bitter white recrimination, social backsliding, and racial violence that blacks began an enormous migration to the urban centers of the North.

Paul Robeson (1898-1976)

Paul Robeson was a champion of the spiritual and work song during his notorious and ultimately tragic life.

A tragic figure in international arts and letters, Paul Robeson was born on April 9, 1898, in Princeton, New Jersey, to a runaway slave named William Drew Robeson and his wife, Maria Louisa (née Bustill), a teacher. Robeson's accomplishments were staggeringly impressive, but he died a scorned, shunned, desperately unhappy man whose public image was that of a Soviet apologist and dangerous crank. Even today Robeson's legacy is split. Some see him as a misunderstood hero—the victim of ignorance, Cold War hysteria, and xenophobia—while others believe him to have been a tragically flawed genius whose radical views could never be reconciled with mainstream American beliefs.

Robeson excelled at whatever he attempted. His athleticism won him a scholarship to Rutgers College, where he was elected Phi Beta Kappa in his junior year and subsequently became valedictorian.

In college Robeson won varsity letters in four sports and was named Rutgers' first All-American in football. He earned a law degree at Columbia University (1923) and entered the practice of law at a New York City firm.

During his tenure at Columbia, Robeson met and married Eslanda Cardozo Goode (1896–1965), who encouraged him to perform in amateur theatrical productions. It wasn't until his disenchantment with the law firm that employed him in 1923, however, that Robeson pursued a full-time career in acting. A stenographer at the firm apparently refused to take Robeson's dictation because of his race. Rather than take an unequivocal stand against racism, the firm's partners tried to skirt the issue by simply providing their new associate with another stenographer. The move mortified rather than mollified Robeson, who promptly quit.

He joined the off-Broadway Provincetown Players, a New York City troupe associated with the playwright Eugene O'Neill, and starred in *All God's Chillun Got Wings* (1924) and *The Emperor Jones* (1925) to tremendous critical acclaim. He was soon starring in larger productions, including *Show Boat* (1928) on Broadway. He also starred in the first film version of *Show Boat* (1936), in which he delivered an unforgettable rendition of "Ol' Man River."

Robeson never considered himself a great actor. He believed his capabilities were limited, and he also believed, with justification, that he and other blacks were hobbled by the limited number of roles available to them. By 1940 Robeson had stopped acting and was appearing in public exclusively as a singer.

Journeys through Europe and Russia in the 1930s brought a dramatic shift in Paul Robeson's sensibilities. He had suffered the full litany of abuses and indignities to which his race has been subject in the United States. He was all too familiar with freight elevators, back doors, second-rate hotels, and segregated accommodations. It was in England that he decided that it was the common people, not the privileged classes, who define the character of a nation. In his autobiography, *Here I Stand*, Robeson wrote that "the common people of all nations are truly brothers in the great family of mankind."

The revelation caused him to switch his repertoire to Negro work songs and spirituals, which he sang mostly to groups of working people and students. He also sang the folk songs of other nations and began learning a number of languages (eventually becoming conversant in about twenty) in order to better communicate with his audiences. He established links with numerous socialist, leftist, and African nationalist groups and came to think of himself as an ambassador in the struggle for social and economic justice for non-whites. In Russia Robeson believed he had found a utopian society completely free of racial prejudice; he felt that it was the only place he could "walk in full human dignity."

Returning to the United States in the late thirties, Robeson became an outspoken supporter of Josef Stalin and an advocate of communism. He began actively agitating for civil rights and for an end to racism; he picketed the White House, started a crusade against lynching, urged Congress to outlaw the racial barriers in professional sports (most notably baseball), and refused to sing before segregated audiences.

During the Cold War, and even after he became aware of Stalin's atrocities, Robeson continued to lobby for socialism and communism, arguing that Stalin's ideas were valid even if his methods were not. Not surprisingly, Robeson was interrogated by Congressional committees during the McCarthy era, and he was maligned by other groups and agencies; the State Department revoked his passport, concert promoters dropped him, and prestigious publications such as *The New York Times* and the *New York Herald-Tribune* chose to ignore his autobiography when it was published in 1958.

By then his career had been ruined. He had become an outcast and an embarrassment even to the groups and associations he had hoped to help. Robeson withdrew into isolation during the sixties and seventies, twice attempting suicide and suffering breakdowns that left him dependent on antidepressant drugs. He died on January 23, 1976, in Philadelphia, after suffering a stroke.

Fisk Jubilee Singers

Immediately following the Civil War, members of a school choir, desperately seeking money to reopen their small, destitute school for freed slaves in Nashville, began performing spirituals for audiences that ordinarily would never have had the opportunity to hear them. The result was astonishing even to the choir members. Audiences in both the United States and Europe embraced the spirituals, and this reception led not only to the resurrection of the Fisk School in Tennessee, but ultimately to the preservation and celebration of hundreds of slave songs through concerts, songbooks, and recordings.

The Fisk School was opened in 1865 or 1866 in an abandoned Union Army barracks in Nashville. It was a project of the American Missionary Association in New York City and the Western Freedmen's Aid Commission in Cincinnati, two of the many agencies that were formed in northern and southern cities to help emancipated blacks move into the mainstream of society. Named for General Clinton B. Fisk (1828–1890) of the Freedmen's Bureau for Tennessee and Kentucky, the school operates today as Fisk University only because of a gamble by its first professor of music and the amazing emotional power of the spiritual.

During the Fisk School's first half-decade, the future didn't look at all bright. A lack of financial support closed the school just six years after it was opened. As a way to raise funds, Fisk's treasurer and professor of music, George L. White (1838–1895), suggested to the board of directors that he take the Fisk choir on a concert tour, an idea the board rejected. Undaunted, White borrowed enough money to get the tour started and in 1871 took a group of nine Fisk students on the road.

The adventure was not without significant risks, the least of which was fi-

George L. White, choirmaster of the Fisk School, proved the universal appeal of spirituals when the Fisk choir sang them to enthusiastic audiences during an 1871 fund-raising concert tour.

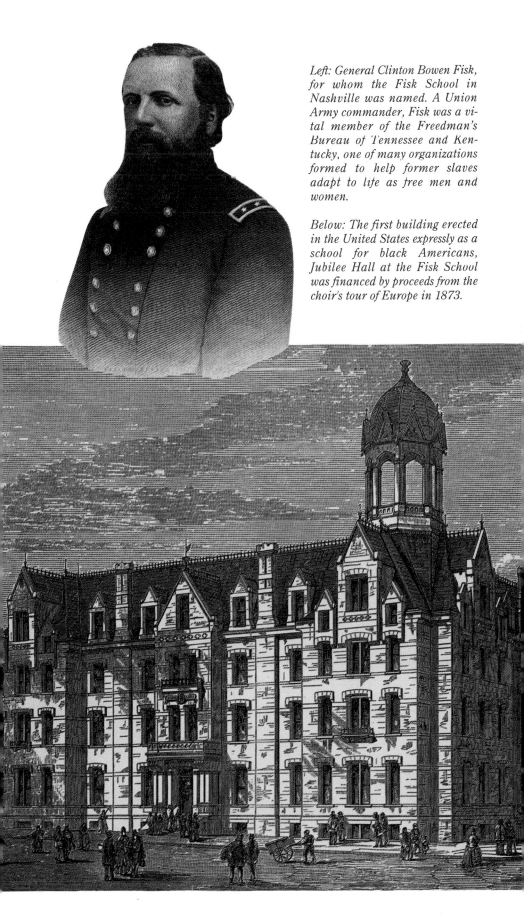

Left: General Clinton Bowen Fisk, for whom the Fisk School in Nashville was named. A Union Army commander, Fisk was a vital member of the Freedman's Bureau of Tennessee and Kentucky, one of many organizations formed to help former slaves adapt to life as free men and women.

Below: The first building erected in the United States expressly as a school for black Americans, Jubilee Hall at the Fisk School was financed by proceeds from the choir's tour of Europe in 1873.

nancial. The group's itinerary took them through the Reconstructionist South at a time when racially based hatred had begun to erupt into Ku Klux Klan violence. Though White was Caucasian, the members of the Fisk choir were black. All but two had formerly been slaves and recalled their bondage vividly. Accommodations were not easy to find, nor was cooperation, assistance, or goodwill. Worse, public reaction to the group's typical program—classical pieces, hymns, and anthems—was lukewarm.

As a teacher at Fisk and the leader of the choir, White was familiar with the spirituals his students would sing when by themselves. Even on that 1871 concert tour his charges would perform their classical repertoire onstage, and later, in their rooms, they would find comfort by singing spirituals. In an inspired move, White decided to include a spiritual in the group's appearance before a convention of Congregational Church ministers in Oberlin, Ohio. Near the end of their program on November 15, the Fisk Singers performed "Steal Away to Jesus"; the response was overwhelmingly enthusiastic. Without hesitation, White shifted the musical thrust of the remaining appearances to spirituals, impressing audiences in New York, throughout New England, and in the White House, where President Ulysses S. Grant heard the choir sing. The excursion was an artistic and financial success. The choir

The Fisk Jubilee Singers of 1873. These are the young men and women who took their repertoire of spirituals to Europe, appearing before Queen Victoria in London and before other influential persons on the European continent.

brought back more than twenty thousand dollars, which was used to buy forty-five acres of land, the present site of Fisk University. Just as significantly, the Fisk Jubilee Singers introduced spirituals—slave songs—to audiences who had never before heard them, and would find them impossible to forget.

A subsequent tour of Europe in 1873 included an appearance before Queen Victoria, who was so taken with the performance that she commissioned a portrait of the Fisk Jubilee Singers from her court painter, Edmund Havel. The group raised $150,000 on that European tour, enough to build Jubilee Hall, a solid Victorian structure that was the first permanent building erected in the United States for the purpose of educating black students. The Havel portrait of the eleven students who took part in the 1873 tour now hangs in Jubilee Hall's auditorium.

Not surprisingly, other institutions quickly followed Fisk's lead and formed choirs that specialized in performing spirituals. Hampton Institute in Virginia and Booker T. Washington's Tuskegee Institute in Alabama were two famous examples, but literally hundreds of other less well known institutions also got involved. What had begun as a startling commercial success soon became a keen competition for audiences. The result was the transformation of the spiritual from a little-known ethnic song form into sophisticated choral music, often specifically tailored for concert perfofmances.

Choir directors, their choirs brimming with trained voices, eventually succumbed to the temptation to "improve" spirituals, both as an artistic challenge and to keep audiences interested. Hampton College choir director Thomas P. Fenner (1829–1912) addressed this temptation in his

Thomas Fenner, choirmaster of the Hampton Institute in Virginia, made "improvements" to spirituals, hoping to broaden their appeal.

The Hampton Institute Singers.

VIRGINIA HALL.—*Now being erected.*

CONCERT BY THE
HAMPTON COLORED STUDENTS !
PROGRAMME.

PART ONE.

1. DON'T YE VIEW THAT SHIP A COME SAILING.
2. VIEW DE LAND, VIEW DE LAND.
   There is a tree in paradise
   The christian calls dat tree of life,
   I spect's to eat de fruit right off o' dat tree,
   If busy ole Satan will let-a-me be.
3. KEEP ME FROM SINKING DOWN
   I'll tell you what I mean to die,
   I mean to go to Heaven too.
4. MY LORD DELIVERED DANIEL.
   Oh Daniel cast in de lion's den,
   He prayed both night and day;
   The angel came from Galilee
   And looked de lion's jaw.
5. THE OLD SLAVE'S FAREWELL.
   Oh boys, carry me 'long,
   Carry me till I die
   Gwoine git down to de burying ground—
   Massa, don't you cry.
6. MY BRETHREN, DON'T GET WEARY.

PART TWO.

1. OH, DE OLE ARK A MOVING ALONG.
   Jess wait a little while, I'm gwine to tell ye 'bout de ole Ark.
2. SOME 'O DESE MORNINGS.
   Gwine to see my mother some o' dese mornings,
   Hope I'll jine de band.
3. THE LITTLE OCTOROON.
   Glory, glory, how the freedmen sang,
   Glory, glory, how the old wools rang.
4. HUMBLE YESELF, DE BELL DUN RING.
   My sister, my sister, oh how do you do,
   I come by de heaven like a wandering Jew—
   I touch a one story and de whole heaven sing,
   Walk in, walk in, de bell don ring.
5. OH SWING LOW, SWEET CHARIOT.
   With (Good News, the Chariot's coming.)
6. OH, WAEN'T DAT A WIDE RIBER.

CHARLES A. J. FARRAR, STEAM JOB PRINTER, Elson Building, Jamaica Plain, Mass.

Reverend Charles Albert Tindley (1851–1933)

One of only a handful of composers upon whose work gospel music was built, Charles Albert Tindley was the son of a slave named Charles Tindley and a free black woman named Hester Miller Tindley. His humble birth on July 7, 1851, in Berlin, Maryland, on the Eastern Shore farm of Joseph Bridell—the man who owned his father—was the beginning of a remarkable life of achievement as a Methodist Episcopal churchman and composer of religious music.

Tindley was not a prolific composer, but the songs he wrote, such as "I'll Overcome Some Day" (1901), "Stand By Me" (1905), and "We'll Understand It Better By and By" (1905), were widely admired in his lifetime, and many of his songs remain popular today. Thomas A. Dorsey, the "Father of Gospel Music," freely credited Tindley's influence, as did other major gospel composers who came later, such as the Reverend William Herbert Brewster. Tindley is credited by many as the first person to write down gospel songs with both music and lyrics included.

Tindley was an effective and progressive cleric whose ministries worked to build lives as well as save souls. He wrote music mostly to augment his powerful sermons, whose themes very often touched on the need for struggle and perseverance on life's rocky road. (These prototypes of gospel music were called tabernacle songs, which focused on a single theme and featured a call-and-response interaction between the soloist and chorus.) His messages were so compelling and so skillfully and fervently delivered that people of all races and socio-economic backgrounds would attend his sermons. Tindley's ministry, from all accounts, was open to all and did not cater to any particular class or color.

Tindley was a masterful organizer and a compassionate realist who knew that before souls could be saved, mouths needed to be fed. The Tindley Temple relief programs became a model for what are now common practices in many urban churches: outreach programs to help struggling members cope with their hard lives and to survive. The members of Tindley's church were mostly former slaves and descendants of slaves who were fleeing the many torments of Reconstruction in the rural South. They benefited from the temple's Depression-era soup kitchens; its political action committees; its educational and job training efforts; the Mt. Calvary Building and Loan Society, which helped them to finance homes of their own; and many of the other programs organized by Tindley, whose own early life personified the kind of hardship that later informed his sermons about struggle and reward.

With no formal education, he taught himself to read by studying newspapers and the Bible. He married Daisy Henry at the age of seventeen, and the pair moved to Philadelphia around 1875, hoping for a better life. There Tindley worked with masons, attending school at night. He also contributed time as a sexton, helping to maintain the Bainbridge Street Methodist Episcopal Church (known then as the John Wesley M.E. Church, renamed Tindley Temple when it was rebuilt). It was during this period that Tindley decided upon a church career, and in 1885 he took and passed the examination to qualify as a minister, entering the Methodist Episcopal ministry with an assignment in Cape May, New Jersey.

One of Tindley's subsequent early ministries was at the Ezion Methodist Episcopal Church in Wilmington, Delaware. It was at Ezion almost seventy years earlier (1822) that a hymn book had been published exclusively for a black congregation by the Reverend Peter Spencer. That hymnal was only the second of its kind; it was preceded by the 1801 publication of Richard Allen's hymnal for the African Methodist Episcopal Church in Philadelphia. The tradition of hymns and song at Ezion and their effect as an uplifting ingredient in worship services were not lost on Tindley, whose own compositions became only part of a rich musical tradition at Tindley Temple. Music was part of the fabric of worship there, from Handel's *Messiah* at Christmastime to the joyful cacophony of the gospel groups Tindley himself organized and trained. In 1922 he formed the Tindley Gospel Singers, which comprised seven men from the congregation. Tindley would often punctuate his own sermons with excerpts from published hymns or the gospel songs he had written.

In 1902 Tindley was named pastor of the same Philadelphia church, Bainbridge Street Methodist Episcopal, at which he had earlier toiled as sexton. He built Bainbridge Street into a major congregation during his thirty-one years at the pulpit; membership rose to more than ten thousand. Easter and Christmas services were often held in rented stadiums to accommodate the thousands who wished to attend. Despite the obvious popular support for the pastor, the construction of a larger church that was to become Tindley Temple was fraught with financial problems that nearly shut down Tindley's ministry.

The new church building was finally completed in 1924. Tindley's satisfaction with the accomplishment was tragically overshadowed, however, by the death of his wife, Daisy, practically on the eve of the Christmas Eve dedication ceremony. Throughout that decade and into the thirties, financial shortfalls and threatened foreclosures took their toll on Tindley's health and his once boundless energy. Nonetheless, he persisted in his duties and responsibilities to his church and its members. Early in 1933 a foot injury escalated into gangrene, and on July 26 of that year, Tindley died.

Unfortunately there are no recordings of Tindley's sermons, which by all accounts were tremendously moving and powerful. Accounts of his many accomplishments as a preacher, organizer, and social force are mostly anecdotal, based on the recollections of colleagues and friends. His gospel songs live on, however, and he will always be remembered for those contributions to the repertoire. Tindley's music will offer future generations the same important lessons about struggle and perseverance that inspired the members of his original flock.

introduction to an 1874 collection of spirituals called *Cabin and Plantation Songs*. He concluded that only two things could legitimately be done with spirituals: they could be performed and preserved in their "rude simplicity" or they could be "developed" without damaging their original character. Fenner opted for the latter, and the spirituals in *Cabin and Plantation Songs* contained vocal harmonies and lyrics that were not present in the originals.

The "development" of spirituals became widespread, particularly among academic choirs. Classical European vocal harmonies were added, as were strict Western tempos and meters. Enunciation became important, and lyrics were "cleaned up"—the patois of illiterate slaves was changed to words that were more understandable. It was common for lyrics to be added or changed at the whim of a choir master. As a result, spirituals took on a completely different sound from their origins as primal cadences in the Brush Arbor Meetings and plantation work gangs.

Jubilee Quartets

The "academic" spiritual style was a big influence on what came to be known as jubilee quartet singing. These groups, usually based in a particular community, generally sang spirituals and contemporary songs in much the same way as the university choirs, but quickly updated their approach to include dramatically innovative vocal solos, particularly by lead tenor and bass voices. The Golden Gate Jubilee Quartet was among the many to emerge from the Tidewater, Virginia, area; with the Hampton Institute nearby, Tidewater was a fertile center of jubilee quartet singing, as was Jefferson County, Alabama, the home of the Tuskegee Institute.

In the 1930s, the jubilee quartets evolved into gospel quartets, with their lead singers "working" a congregation much as a preacher would. The forties and fifties saw the emergence of such great gospel groups as the Swan Silvertones, the Swanee Quintet, the Dixie Hummingbirds, the Five Blind Boys (of both Alabama and Jackson, Mississippi), the Harmonizing Four, and the Soul Stirrers. These were only several of the thousands that sang and composed in the community gospel tradition, contributing volumes to the literature of gospel music.

One of gospel's earliest professional groups, The Swan Silvertones were a natural extension of the informal community group tradition that was itself an imitation and outgrowth of jubilee quartet singing.

Musical disciples of the Soul Stirrers, the Dixie Hummingbirds (opposite page) and the Original Five Blind Boys of Mississippi (below), also known as the Jackson Harmoneers, specialized in sophisticated a cappella harmonizing. Tremendously popular in the thirties and forties, both groups sang gospel music primarily in a religious context, but also performed at clubs and other secular venues.

Pentecostal Revival

While the institute choirs and jubilee quartets were busy trans-
forming spirituals, there was great drama unfolding in the store-
front temples and Pentecostal congregations that were opening up
in rural communities and in the new black neighborhoods of the
nation's cities. These were sometimes called holiness, or sanctified, churches, and their members were active, not passive worshipers. In the ceremonies of these denominations music played
the vital role of summoning up spirit possession in members of the
congregation. These holiness churches were the birthplace of congregational gospel. Their "shout" songs and "witness" rituals, in
which worshipers were encouraged to let the spirit of Christ take
possession of their bodies, were the foundations of modern gospel
music. During the services, in response to the exhortations of the
preacher and propelled by percussive music, congregants would
shout and sing, often writhing in their seats or twirling in the aisles
as if possessed. It was in the Pentecostal churches around the turn
of the century that slave music began to give way to both spontaneous and rehearsed songs, which eventually became the repertoire of gospel.

Thomas Andrew Dorsey (1899–1993)

It may seem ironic that a barrelhouse blues pianist and well-known
rake would end up remembered as the "Father of Gospel," but that's
exactly the case with Thomas Andrew Dorsey. A lanky Georgian
whose father was an itinerant Baptist preacher, Dorsey spent his
young manhood playing blues piano in dancehalls and bars, earning
the nicknames "Barrelhouse Tom" and "Georgia Tom." He went on
the road as pianist and musical director for such spicy blues singers
as Gertrude "Ma" Rainey (1886–1939) and Bessie Smith (1894–1937),
and, in collaboration with guitarist Tampa Red (Hudson Whittaker),
penned a number of very suggestive and very successful blues hits,
including "It's Tight Like That," and "Pat That Bread."

Never apologetic for the wanderlust of his youth, Dorsey was
above all else a determined musician who hustled to promote his

Opposite page : The Holy Rollers, *a painting by Morton Roberts, shows the abandon*
of "spirit possession" common in Pentecostal and "holiness" churches.

Georgia Tom

As a young man, Thomas A. Dorsey was known as "Georgia Tom." An aggressive and ambitious songwriter, he was an accompanist for such bawdy blues singers as Ma Rainey and Bessie Smith.

music wherever he could, blithely switching from one style to another if such a change could sell a song or get him a job. Nevertheless he spent the majority of his life as a tireless exponent and organizer of gospel music, composing more than five hundred gospel songs, including what is perhaps the most universally familiar gospel number, "Precious Lord, Take My Hand," composed in what must have been the most dismal moments of Dorsey's life—the days in 1932 following the death of his wife (in childbirth) and the subsequent death of his newborn child. "Precious Lord" was the song the Reverend Martin Luther King, Jr., asked to hear just moments before his assassination, and immediately thereafter it became an anthem of the Civil Rights movement.

Thomas A. Dorsey with Mahalia Jackson, one of the singers whom Dorsey helped and who recorded stirring versions of many of his gospel songs.

Dorsey was writing gospel music as early as 1919, trying to sell it to this congregation or that, while at the same time playing joints and dives as "Georgia Tom," the rollicking blues pianist. Moving first to Atlanta and then to Chicago in what was a typical path for many blacks (and musicians in particular) during and after Reconstruction, Dorsey wrote "If You See My Savior," an acknowledged masterpiece of gospel, in 1926. He created a sensation with the song four years later at the 1930 Jubilee Meeting of the

National Baptist Convention, a meeting that according to many gospel historians was the closest event as any to gospel's official moment of birth.

The Baptist Convention had heard and sanctioned religious music long before Dorsey's 1930 visit. In 1893 it had published William Henry Sherwood's "Mountain Top Dwelling" and in 1919 had enthusiastically received Lucie Eddie Campbell's "Something Within." Other composers had contributed quite a lot of work to

the musical repertoire of gospel; among these were Charles Price Jones, who in 1899 introduced "Where Shall I Be When the First Trumpet Sounds," and the Reverend Charles Albert Tindley, who began publishing his devout Protestant hymns in 1901. But the thoughtful, reverent work of these composers had been overshadowed in the 1920s by the wild abandon of the sanctified and holiness churches, whose music was rattling rafters in the churches of many cities, to the horror of the mainline denominations.

A composer, evangelist, and publisher, Thomas A. Dorsey also formed and led his own gospel choir, the Dorsey Gospel Singers, in the 1930s.

Lucie Eddie Campbell Williams (1885–1963)

Born on April 30, 1885, on a train just outside her family's hometown of Duck Hill, Mississippi, Lucie Campbell never knew her father, Burrell, who was killed in a train accident as he rushed home from his railroad job to see his newborn daughter. The tragedy prompted Lucie's mother, Isabella Wilkerson Campbell, to move her eleven sons and daughters to a place of greater opportunity; she chose Memphis, where the family settled around 1887. There Isabella Campbell worked at a number of domestic jobs to assure that her children were given a reasonably comfortable life; she was especially determined that they all receive an education. Isabella Campbell was able to afford music lessons for her eldest daughter, Lora, and because of Lucie's keen interest, Isabella ended up getting two lessons for the price of one: Lucie would listen to her sister's lessons from an adjoining room, later repeating what she had heard. In this way, Lucie Campbell taught herself the rudiments of piano playing and composition.

The rancorous 1915 split in the black Baptist church, caused by a struggle for control of its Publishing Board, brought Lucie Campbell into the upper echelons. The festering dispute over how that enterprise ought to be administered led the Reverend Richard Henry Boyd (1843–1922) to form a breakaway faction, which eventually organized itself in Chicago's Salem Baptist Church. Boyd's decision to set up the Publishing Board in his own name had been at the root of the dispute; his new church took the enterprise with it, leaving the National Baptist

Lucie Campbell, the first woman to contribute significantly as a composer of gospel music, copyrighted her first songs in 1919. By then she was a teacher of English and American history at Booker T. Washington High School in Memphis, a job she had taken when she was fourteen. She was also music director of the Baptist Training Union Congress in 1919, and was on her way to becoming a major force in the National Baptist Convention (which published one of Campbell's 1919 songs, "The Lord Is My Shepherd," in the 1921 debut of its *Gospel Pearls* hymnal). Lucie Campbell would rise to prominence as the composer of more than one hundred gospel songs, including standards such as "He'll Understand; He'll Say, 'Well Done'" (1933); through these contributions, she became a defining presence in the development of gospel music in its formative years.

Convention without a publishing wing. The leadership of the original church called a congress in Memphis the following year to assess the damage and make plans for the future. Because of her reputation as a tireless worker, Lucie Campbell was selected as one of the nine organizers of that important event.

The decision to appoint Campbell was inspired. She used her extraordinary organizational skills to plan and stage musicales, pageants, and concerts that elevated the mood of the delegates and oiled the wheels of what otherwise might have been a grim and grinding convention. Many of the songs performed during the 1916 congress were Campbell's own compositions, and they were taken back by delegates to churches across the land, becoming a permanent part of each denomination's musical repertoire. Lucie Campbell was soon appointed to the board that was formed to select music for inclusion in the church's hymnals and songbooks, and she eventually became the Training Union's music director.

Campbell's own compositions evolved gradually from hymns to full-blown gospel songs, which she preferred to be sung in the European classical style rather than in the uninhibited fashion of Pentecostal groups. She is credited with inventing a gospel style that employed 3/4 time, the "gospel waltz," which was appropriated in the 1950s by Ray Charles, among others. Although stern and musically demanding, Campbell was not reluctant to experiment with different musical styles, including "lining-hymns," in which a preacher or deacon states or sings a verse that the congregation then repeats in song. "Something Within" (1919) and "A Sinner Like Me" (1952) are two examples of lining-hymns. The latter is also considered a "gospel bal-lad," a slow, aching form to which Campbell also contributed.

Despite her influence in the National Baptist Convention, Campbell's relationships with individual officials of the church were not always harmonious. She was a proud and temperamental woman who was disturbed by what she considered the patronizing attitude of the male leadership toward women, especially women like herself who contributed so much to the organization. Not surprisingly, women were given high visibility but no real power in administrating the denomination. It was a situation that Campbell challenged from time to time. Those challenges often failed, sometimes disastrously. She was thrown out of two Memphis congregations as the result of her power struggles with their leadership; the Metropolitan Baptist Church ejected her when she tried to block the appointment of a pastor of whom she did not approve, and the Central Baptist Church threw her out for refusing to end a feud with a deacon who had displeased her.

Tempted to leave church work, Campbell instead decided to do what she could to subdue her rancor. She continued to write, promote, and organize. In a rare victory over the patriarchal leadership, Campbell succeeded in reversing a decision to bar the flamboyant Clara Ward Singers from singing at a congress in the early 1950s.

In 1960 Lucie Campbell married her lifelong friend and fellow teacher, the Reverend C. R. Williams. She was seventy-five years old at the time. She died two years later in Nashville, having served a remarkable forty-seven years as a music director in the National Baptist Convention and contributed nearly a lifetime to the development and exposition of gospel music.

Despite his blues experience and his jazz work as leader of a recording outfit called Texas Tommy and Friends, Dorsey was not keen on the undisciplined and raucous nature of the singing in the sanctified churches. He observed at one point that a number of choirs exhibited "too many embellishments that may be mistaken for spirit." He criticized "loud vociferous singing, uninspired gesticulations, or self-incurred spasms of the body." He held that "shouting, running, and crying out" was acceptable, but only "if the Holy Spirit comes upon one." He did not sanction "going to get the Spirit before it comes." Remarkably, it was the popularity of those wilder ceremonies that resulted in the eventual acceptance of gospel singing in the major churches. In the 1920s there were plenty of recordings of sanctified shouters and other "holy rollers" whose mere presence helped lessen the solemnity that was expected in most houses of worship. It was a battle that Dorsey himself had to fight; his uptempo, almost ragtime blues arrangements irritated quite a few pastors who were evidently offended by the music's lack of decorum.

Dorsey was as prolific as Bach or Mozart and was also a tireless organizer, promoter, and entrepreneur—all of which contributed to his importance in the birth and nurturing of gospel music. Above all it is the elegance, honesty, and poetry of his devotionals that have endured and that continue to touch and inspire people everywhere; Dorsey characteristically wrote satisfying songs with lyrics rich in spiritual imagery and optimism that were easy for almost everyone to sing. That was his gift and his art.

Among Dorsey's many remarkable promotional accomplishments was the formation of the first female gospel quartet and choir in 1931. With several other musicians, including a longtime colleague, the singer Sallie Martin (1896–1988), Dorsey founded the first National Convention of Gospel Choirs and Choruses in 1932. With Martin's considerable assistance, he opened and operated the first gospel publishing company, Dorsey House, in Chicago, that same year. Never shy about commercial matters, Dorsey staged the first paid-admission gospel concert in Chicago in 1936; this show featured performances by Roberta Martin and Sallie Martin (the two were not related). Dorsey was also one of the primary engineers of the "gospel highway," the well-traveled evangelical routes that brought gospel to many churches (black and white) throughout the country.

Thomas A. Dorsey (above), the "Father of Gospel Music," exhorts a congregation to sing in praise of God, circa 1979. Roberta Martin (second from left, below) formed and led one of gospel's hardest-working and most influential groups, the Roberta Martin Singers. Famous around the world, Martin's group toured frequently and extensively and became the standard by which other gospel groups of the time were judged.

Roberta Martin (1907–1969)

the years, the Martin Singers traveled hundreds of thousands of miles, on several continents, performing thousands of concerts before millions of listeners. Their musical and evangelical impact was incalculable; they were warmly received wherever they went.

Born on February 12, 1907, in Helena, Arkansas, Roberta Evelyn Winston showed an early interest in music, and also a great aptitude for it. As a toddler she would sit at the piano and plunk out recognizable tunes. As a youngster she became the piano pupil of her sister-in-law, learning the works of such composers as Brahms, Beethoven, and Chopin. Roberta seemed destined to become a classical musician, or at the very least a professional accompanist.

Anna and William Winston and their six children moved to Chicago when Roberta was ten. After graduating from Wendell Phillips High School, Martin became the pianist for a youth choir at the Ebenezer Baptist Church and was soon working with Thomas A. Dorsey, the "Father of Gospel Music." Both Dorsey and the choir's gospel arranger, Theodore R. Frye (1899–1963), took an interest in Martin, guiding her early career. Both men would benefit considerably from Martin's energy and ambition as her career flourished. In 1933, at the age of twenty-six, Martin organized the Martin-Frye Quartet, a gospel group that three years later became the Roberta Martin

Roberta Martin's contributions to gospel music were vast. She helped popularize the form in its early days, and was the originator of the "Roberta Martin sound," a distinctive, refined sensibility that imbued her songs and arrangements with a dramatic sophistication rarely matched. One of the pioneers who wrote and promoted gospel music in the thirties, Martin quickly became a model for her contemporaries and an inspiration to other musicians through her innovations in arrangement, singing, and piano technique. She also became a significant political and commercial force as founder of a gospel music publishing company that became the largest in Chicago.

Martin's most visible legacy—the Roberta Martin Singers—introduced a dynamic new sound to gospel, combining male and female voices for the first time in striking contrast to the traditional all-male and all-female gospel quartets and groups of the twenties and thirties. Over

Singers. She also organized many of the gospel groups and choirs that accompanied Dorsey on his "gospel highway" campaigns, traveling from tent to church to stadium in the thirties and forties, spreading the gospel message.

In 1939 Martin opened the Roberta Martin Studio of Music, a gospel publishing enterprise that soon became the largest in Chicago and one of the most influential in the United States. Her mentor in that business was Dorsey, who operated his own publishing house in Chicago, administered by his longtime colleague Sallie Martin. In its heyday, Martin's publishing company sold and distributed sheet music of her songs and her arrangements to practically every black church in the United States. She also nurtured a thriving trade in the music of other gospel composers, becoming a major force in the field in more ways than one.

Martin wrote about seventy gospel songs, and never hesitated to perform and promote music written by others. For example, the Gloria Griffin song "God Specializes" was without a doubt the most popular piece performed by the Roberta Martin Singers. Martin's elegant arrangements and the distinctive, disciplined performances of the choirs she formed, especially the Roberta Martin Singers, won praise and tremendous respect and admiration from audiences and colleagues alike. By the mid-fifties, the Roberta Martin Singers were known around the world and were considered the finest gospel ensemble of the day. Quartets and choirs in black churches everywhere followed their example and emulated their performance style, using records and concert appearances for guidance. The Roberta Martin Singers began recording in the forties on the Apollo label, but the bulk of their music was issued by Savoy from the mid-fifties to the mid-sixties.

One of the hardest-working gospel groups ever, the Roberta Martin Singers traveled widely and frequently as part of the gospel and revival movement that spread east from Chicago, and then out to the west coast. They headlined sold-out shows in concert halls, in stadiums, and at festivals. They appeared practically everywhere, from California to Griffith Stadium in Washington, D.C., to Randall's Island in New York City. A 1963 concert in New York City's Coliseum drew thousands to a show that also featured Mahalia Jackson and the Reverend James Cleveland. Other New York City venues that hosted them include Madison Square Garden and Carnegie Hall. In 1967 the ensemble appeared at the Spoleto Festival of Two Worlds in Italy, the only gospel group invited to a festival that was otherwise dedicated to classical music. They sold out Wrigley Field in Chicago for an anniversary appearance, and in a 1974 reunion, they headlined a sold-out gospel extravaganza at Detroit's Cobo Arena.

Roberta Martin toured and performed with her singers through the forties. She then devoted herself to writing and arranging music, and running the publishing company. Except for a few special concerts, the Roberta Martin Singers had retired by the end of the sixties. Roberta Martin herself died on January 18, 1969, after a long illness. Her death signaled the close of an amazing and powerful chapter in the history of gospel music. Recognizing the magnitude of the loss, more than fifty thousand people turned out for Martin's memorial service, and one Chicago newspaper proclaimed her "an institution in her own time."

Clara Ward's association with the gospel composer Reverend William Herbert Brewster brought new sophistication and depth to gospel music in the 1950s. A composer in her own right, Ward recorded quite a few Brewster compositions with the Clara Ward Singers, and Ward's Philadelphia publishing company, Ward's House of Music, was Brewster's primary publisher.

Dorsey was mentor to the first generation of gospel singers, many of whom will always be remembered for their extraordinary gifts and talent. He trained and encouraged the likes of Roberta and Sallie Martin, Clara Ward (1924–1973), and Mahalia Jackson. Through the wide distribution of his music, Dorsey influenced untold thousands of other singers and writers (Elvis Presley [1935–1977] and Red Foley [1910–1968] both had hits with their arrangements of his "Peace in the Valley"). Rock and pop music owe more to the blues and gospel traditions than to any other influence. Dorsey's Pilgrim Baptist Church at 33rd Street and Indiana Avenue in Chicago was a wellspring—some say the source—of gospel music.

The progress of gospel has been relentless since Dorsey's groundbreaking work in the 1930s. It is no surprise that a musical form with the powerful emotional content of gospel immediately interested entertainment moguls whose business it is to translate that kind of promise into record sales. Almost from the outset there was trade in gospel among small specialty and "ethnic" labels, whose clientele was almost exclusively black. While the questions of race and the dubious commercial appeal of religious music initially hobbled the enthusiasm of the major record labels to capitalize on the form, there was also a reluctance on the part of gospel singers themselves to get into show business. Many faced considerable pressure from family, peers, and pastors not to sully what was often perceived as a high calling and a sacred duty. In fact, the prevailing view in most black churches was that secular appearances by gospel performers were blasphemous. The music eventually escaped, however, and was spread by promoters both divine and devilish through conduits and corridors both sacred and secular; in the end it got around mostly on its own considerable merit.

Gospel as Popular Music

The legendary record producer, talent scout, and jazz critic John Hammond (1910–1987) was an early and vigorous proponent of gospel music, dedicating many years to the task of showcasing the potent new music to a wide and diverse audience. In 1938 he organized a show at Carnegie Hall in New York City called "From Spirituals to Swing" that featured spirituals, gospel, blues, and jazz. Hammond hired Mitchell's Christian Singers to perform the spiri-

The Original Carter Family

A trio of homesteaders from the Clinch Mountain area of western Virginia, the Carters are best remembered as the founding family of American country music. Their unadorned, traditional singing style celebrated the unadorned, traditional lives of other rural homesteaders and small-town Americans whose stories they told. More than three hundred Carter Family songs survive as a historic, recorded archive of the American folk tradition. A few of those songs, such as "On the Rock Where Moses Stood," are "white gospel" renditions of Protestant hymns.

Like many of their Clinch Mountain neighbors, the Carters were devout Christians whose lives were imbued at an early age with gospel and scripture. Alvin Pleasant Delaney Carter (1891–1960) was born in mid-December near Maces Springs, Virginia. One of Robert and Mollie Carter's nine children, A.P., as he came to be called, was raised on heavy doses of music and religion. He could be heard singing in local church quartets, his tremulous bass voice strengthening into the instrument that would eventually become familiar to millions.

A.P. Carter married Sara Dougherty (1898–1979) of nearby Copper Creek, Virginia, in 1915, and the pair settled near Maces Springs, continuing the routine familiar to each: they would sing and play music as the spirit moved them,

Maybelle, Sara, and A.P. Carter, the Original Carter Family.

Sara's autoharp, banjo, or guitar providing the rhythm that supported her strong alto voice and A.P.'s bass. Sara's cousin, Maybelle Addington (1909–1978), would occasionally contribute a guitar accompaniment.

A 1928 audition in Bristol, Virginia, for New York record producer Ralph Peer eventually led to stardom for the Carters. Much of what they recorded, songs such as "Will the Circle be Unbroken," was authentic folk or traditional music handed down for generations. Some songs were based on folk tunes that had been jumbled in their journey through time (A.P. would rewrite lyrics, or compose his own if people's recollections were only partial). Other songs were religious in nature, taken from hymnals or reconstructed from memory. Sara and

Mother Maybelle Carter and her daughters June, Helen, and Anita began performing together after the Original Carter Family disbanded.

Maybelle worked up the arrangements, and the three together would negotiate how the material would be performed.

Even if their renditions were sometimes hybrid, the Carters maintained a vocal and instrumental integrity in their music, rarely succumbing to popular trends. It is because of that integrity and consistency that their music is considered such a valuable historical resource. These traits also endeared the Carters to millions of listeners who, finding their expectations and dreams shattered during the Great Depression, heard with new poignancy about simpler, happier, more secure times, in such songs as "The Little Poplar Log House" and "Homestead on the Farm."

The success of their records put the Carter Family on the road, and they performed as a unit until 1943, most successfully after a three-year stint on XERA, a "border radio" station in Mexico, just across the line from Del Rio, Texas. In later years, country talents from Waylon Jennings and Chet Atkins to George Jones and Woody Guthrie would tell of listening to the Carter Family over XERA, often going out of their way to do so.

A.P. and Sara Carter separated in 1933. Even though they lived apart, the Carter Family continued to appear together until Sara moved to California in 1942 with her new husband, A.P.'s cousin Coy Bayes. After the Carter Family disbanded, A.P. returned to Maces Springs to work his farm, eventually opening a grocery store. In the early fifties, a brief attempt at a comeback that included their children, Joe and Janette Carter, fizzled, and in 1956 each retired, never again to perform professionally.

Maybelle and her three daughters, June, Helen, and Anita, continued to perform as The Carter Sisters and Mother Maybelle. In a few short years they were the toast of Nashville, becoming regulars on the Grand Ole Opry in 1950. In 1961, June Carter joined Johnny Cash's "Road Show." As the folk revival movement of the sixties gathered momentum, Cash hired Maybelle, Anita, and Helen, too. The family made regular appearances on Cash's national TV show in the sixties, and June, after her divorce from country singer Carl Smith, married Johnny Cash in 1968.

A.P. Carter's heart failed on November 7, 1960, in Maces Springs; Maybelle died on October 23, 1978, in Madison, Tennessee; and Sara died a short time later in Lodi, California, on January 8, 1979.

Reverend William Herbert Brewster (1897–1987)

A great innovator in gospel music's developmental period, during the thirties and forties, William Herbert Brewster was also a preacher and biblical scholar whose encyclopedic knowledge of both the Old and New testaments was gained largely through personal exploration of scripture. He would very often incorporate arcane Old Testament information into his songs, stumping other preachers and further distinguishing his already uncommonly sophisticated lyrics. Brewster's musical knowledge was also gained mostly on his own initiative. He was trained in shape-note singing, but he taught himself the rudiments of piano and began singing hymns and gospel songs principally because it was something a preacher was expected to do.

Born on a plantation east of Memphis, William Brewster is credited with composing more than two hundred gospel songs during his long lifetime. The exact number is uncertain because of his spontaneous writing style and his early lack of concern about whether or not the music was transcribed. Later in his career, Brewster became a savvy and aggressive promoter of his music, but as a youngster and as a young man, he was less careful. Brewster would very often conceive a complete work in his mind and teach it to a soloist or choir; only eventually (if at all) would the music be written down by an arranger or someone else familiar with notation.

Distinguished as a composer of "recitative and aria" songs, Brewster also composed "sacred pageants," "gospel ballads," "gospel waltzes," "jubilees," and music in a style of gospel called "vamp." Vamp used extensive repetition, a device heard in many traditional and folk songs, to build excitement and drive home a message. Also called "cumulative songs," vamps have parallels in other genres; the familiar Christmas carol "The Twelve Days of Christmas" is a good example. Closer to the musical mark, the traditional song "Children Go Where I Send Thee" is a vamp in which God's children are sent out one by one, two by two, three by three, and so on, to the following refrain:

> One for the little bitty baby
> Two for Paul and Silas
> Three for the Hebrew Children. . .
> Ten for the Ten Commandments

"Move On Up a Little Higher" (1946) is Brewster's best-known vamp. Recorded by Mahalia Jackson in the year it was written, it became the first gospel song to sell more than a million records, establishing Jackson's international career. Other great gospel soloists and groups also benefited professionally from Brewster's music: the Soul Stirrers had a hit in 1946 with "Lord I've Tried" (Claude Jeter and the Swan Silvertones had a hit with the same song in 1947); Clara Ward and Marion Williams had a million-plus hit with the gospel waltz "Surely God Is Able" (1949); Clara Ward had success with "How I Got Over" (1951). Many other prominent gospel singers, Queen C. Anderson (for whom Brewster wrote many of his songs), Sam Cooke of the Soul Stirrers, and Sister Rosetta Tharpe among them, would regularly visit Brewster's East Trigg Baptist Church in Memphis looking for material. His songs became, and remain, staples in the gospel repertoire.

Brewster also authored sacred pageants. These religious musicals—passion plays, really—were not new, but Brewster was the first writer to compose and incorporate gospel music as an organic part of the production. Earlier pageants had been "written around" music that already existed. When Brewster's "From Auction Block to Glory" debuted at the 1941 National Baptist Convention, however, it was the first gospel pageant to be written expressly as such. "Auction Block" was enthusiastically received and the convention immediately named Brewster head of its drama department.

That pageant was one of many written by Brewster, a list of which includes "These Our Children," about parental joy; "The Rejected Stone," a passion play; and "Deep Dark Waters," about the destructiveness of drug abuse. Pageants became a monthly fixture at Brewster's East Trigg Baptist Church. Ultimately, his body of work had tremendous influence on the work of other black playwrights, especially Langston Hughes and Ossie Davis. Many also saw in Brewster's pageants, some of which were performed as the Civil Rights movement gained momentum, elements that encouraged the struggle for racial equality. Brewster himself said that he took the history of nations and of peoples from the Bible and proved that "racial inferiority was a balloon that could be punctured by the truth . . . that all men are created equal."

tuals and he engaged Sister Rosetta Tharpe (1915–1973), whose only previous appearances had been in black churches, to sing gospel songs. Her skillful blending of gospel and jazz was a big hit with the audience and with critics. The show was so well received that Hammond staged another the following year featuring the Golden Gate Jubilee Quartet. Several years later Hammond organized a nightclub tour for Tharpe, the Golden Gate Quartet, and the Dixie Hummingbirds; this tour was moderately successful, but exposed all the singers to severe criticism from their clergy.

It was quartets and other harmony groups that first got the commercial ball rolling in a big way. In the thirties and forties, thousands of small vocal groups modeled after the academic jubilee quartets of Fisk, Tuskegee, and Hampton sprang up across the country. In the forties, groups like the Mills Brothers and the Ink Spots were clearly gospel-driven, and because of the skillful and pleasing harmonies of that period's vocal groups, the post–World War II years came to be known as the "sweet-gospel" era. It was also during the forties that spectacular recordings were made of quartets, quintets, and sextets such as the Soul Stirrers (which in the fifties became a vehicle for the singer Sam Cooke), The Swan Silvertones (whose tenor, Claude Jeter [1914–   ], still amazes listeners with his mesmerizing vocal gymnastics), the super-smooth Dixie Hummingbirds, the Fairfield Four, the Sensational Nightingales, and the Pilgrim Travelers.

The 1950s ushered in the "hard gospel" groups, such as the Original Five Blind Boys of Alabama, and was the decade in which gospel's "divas"— Mahalia Jackson, Clara Ward, Marion Williams (1927–   ), Roberta Martin, and Della Reese (1931–   ) among them—blossomed. The

The Golden Gate Jubilee Quartet, one of gospel's first professional singing groups, originated in Tidewater, Virginia, home of the Hampton Institute, a fertile source of gospel groups in the jubilee and community traditions.

Unlike most of her contemporaries in the world of gospel, Della Reese did not hesitate to perform for commercial gain; nor did she make apologies. With the Meditation Singers (inset, Reese is at bottom), she appeared at the Copacabana in New York City and at other nightclubs and similar venues.

fifties was also the decade in which gospel performers started to make big money. (A label called Specialty Records was a major source of gospel recordings in the fifties, releasing discs by such talents as The Swan Silvertones, the Soul Stirrers, and James Cleveland.) Popularized even among nonreligious blacks by "inner city" radio stations, gospel music was ubiquitous in black neighborhoods of every American city by the mid-1950s. In addition, it was making inroads around the world. Gospel soloists such as Jackson, Ward, Martin, and Reese appeared in large auditoriums, stadiums, and prestigious concert halls, generally selling them out. These artists became, essentially, full-time performers. Ward and Reese even began appearing in nightclubs and theaters—Clara Ward said her mission in such places was evangelical, while Della Reese made no excuses for her pursuit of fame and creature comforts. Most of the great soloists, however, notably Mahalia Jackson and James Cleveland, did not succumb to the temptations of fame and fortune and maintained their places in the ranks of the army of the Lord.

The Ink Spots (opposite page, top) and the Mills Brothers (right) were primarily vocal entertainers, not gospel singers. Their styles and commercial success, however, owed much to the gospel quartet tradition.

Formed in the 1920s, the Pilgrim Travelers (above) and the Fairfield Four (opposite page, top) were renowned and beloved a cappella gospel groups. Although several of its members are now in their seventies, the Fairfield Four continues to perform today at churches and concerts. Of more recent vintage are the Sensational Nightingales (opposite page, bottom).

Mahalia Jackson (1911–1972)

Mahalia Jackson was gospel's first superstar. She traveled the world as a beloved singer of hymns, spirituals, and gospel songs, introducing their power to audiences of many races. She accompanied the evangelist and "Father of Gospel Music," Thomas A. Dorsey, on the "gospel highway" of tent meetings and revivals. She lent her remarkable talent to the momentous cause of civil rights. She was invited to sing at the inauguration of President John F. Kennedy. Her admirers numbered in the millions but Jackson's outlook was reverent, even pious, and she consistently turned down invitations to sing that were based purely in commercial interest.

Mahalia Jackson was born on October 26, 1911, into a poor New Orleans family, and was raised amid that city's colorful musi-

cal pastiche. As a youngster she was known as the "little girl with the big voice," and she dutifully sang in a local church choir. Her ear was open to the many other kinds of music that wafted regularly throughout the city, especially blues and jazz. Jackson might very well have pursued a career as a singer of the blues, a music she loved, were it not for the discouragement of her devoutly religious family, who considered the blues decadent and constantly urged Mahalia to use her voice only in praise of God.

With aspirations of becoming a nurse, Jackson traveled to Chicago at the age of sixteen and moved in with her aunt Hannah. She worked as a dollar-a-day washerwoman, singing regularly in the choir of her aunt's Greater Salem Baptist Church. Her singing ability was quickly recognized and she was elevated to soloist. Just as quickly she was invited to join a quintet called the Johnson Gospel Singers that in 1930 traveled around the region performing at special church functions such as funerals and revivals. In 1934, for a fee of twenty-five dollars, she made her first recording: "God's Gonna Separate the Wheat From the Tares."

At the height of the Great Depression, Jackson wrestled with the question of how best to earn a living. Lucrative opportunities to sing blues were popping up, but she was torn. Her first husband, Isaac Hockenhull, whom she married in 1936, urged her to get into show business, and it may have been friction over this issue that led to their divorce. Casting about for some kind of sign, she found it in her grandfather's recovery, for which she fervently prayed, from a stroke and coma. In her autobiography, *Moving On Up*, Jackson identified that incident as a defining moment: ". . . that is why He suffered my prayers to be answered—so that nothing would distract me from being a gospel singer."

In 1939 Jackson went on the road with Thomas Dorsey, putting in five years on the gospel highway. She returned to Chicago and opened a beauty parlor and flower shop, continuing to sing in local churches. It was her recording in 1946 of Reverend William Herbert Brewster's song "Move On Up a Little Higher" that brought Mahalia Jackson to the attention of the world. This song became gospel's first million-selling record, and was even played on more than a few non-black radio stations.

The wide acceptance of "Move On Up" put Jackson back on the road. Even as her stature grew she toured the country in an automobile that was big enough for her to sleep in because many hotels would not accommodate African Americans. She kept food in the car to avoid the humiliation of the segregated seating at many restaurants.

Despite the indignities she and other blacks suffered in some parts of the United States, Mahalia Jackson was honored and revered in others. The Chicago writer Studs Terkel invited her to appear regularly on his radio show, and in 1950 she appeared at Carnegie Hall In New York City before an emotional and appreciative audience. In 1956, Jackson appeared at the Newport Jazz Festival in Rhode Island, where she also performed as soloist in a Sunday service at the supremely Waspish Newport Trinity Episcopal Church. By the mid-fifties, Jackson was being called the "Queen of Gospel," and a European and Asian tour won her legions of admirers in France, England, Germany, Denmark, and the fledgling nation of Israel.

In the late fifties and sixties Jackson lent her support to the Civil Rights movement in the United States, participating in the Montgomery bus boycott at the request of the Reverend Martin Luther King, Jr. In the famous 1963 march on Washington, Jackson sang "I Been 'Buked and I Been Scorned" as preamble to the Reverend King's epic "I Have a Dream" address.

Mahalia Jackson recorded eight songs that sold more than one million copies, including "I Believe" and "He's Got the Whole World in His Hands." This sort of success was unprecedented for gospel music, and for a black woman of her era. Jackson's consistent refusal to leave the gospel field for a far more lucrative singing career speaks volumes about her outlook and integrity. Summarizing her philosophy in her autobiography, Jackson said, "gospel music is nothing but . . . spreading the good news. It will last as long as any music because it is sung straight from the human heart. Its future is brighter than a daisy."

Hampered by ill health late in her life, Mahalia Jackson died of a heart attack on January 27, 1972, in Evergreen Park, Illinois.

Soul music, one of gospel's children, is epitomized by the legendary performers James Brown (below) and Ray Charles (bottom). Both men have achieved spectacular artistic and commercial success in soul music, a secular hybrid of gospel. The Reverend Al Green (left) began his career as a gospel singer, briefly lapsed into soul, and has since returned to the gospel fold.

Gospel and Its Godchildren

The explosive growth of soul in the sixties perhaps owes as much to the influence of gospel as it does to the influence of the blues. The children of soul (for example, funk) are likewise indebted to gospel. Superstars of the sixties and seventies, including Ray Charles (for whom The Raelettes generated a call-and-response intensity borrowed directly from the gospel tradition) and Al Green (who began as a gospel singer, fell from grace, and is today a gospel artist again), were avid students of, and often had their roots in, gospel. Musically, many aspects of the popular music of the sixties onward are derived from gospel, including call-and-response and melismatic singing (an ornamental style derived in turn from ancient plainsong) and many rhythmic elements. In addition, many of the textural qualities of the music of these periods is gospel-derived, particularly in the vocals; the multi octave acrobatics of Al Green and the stunning growls, whoops, and grunts of James Brown all have ties to the singing style of the sanctified and holiness services earlier in the century.

The embodiment of the link between gospel and the popular forms that followed is Sam Cooke, a tragic figure in the musical world. Cooke began singing with the Soul Stirrers in 1951, when he was only twenty years old. Following in the footsteps of R.H. Harris, the immensely popular former lead singer for the group, was daunting. Cooke's incredibly well-controlled and beautifully pure voice, however, brought his first audience to its feet. He and the Soul Stirrers went on to become the most popular gospel ensemble of their day.

Cooke, however, with his incredible good looks and smooth, sexy voice, was destined for an even more successful career in popular music. His first pop recordings were released under the name Dale Cook, so as not to upset the religious audience. These recordings proved that there was a viable meeting ground for the exalted intensity of gospel and the secular finger popping of rhythm and blues. Throughout his pop career, which extended from 1957 to his untimely and unseemly death in 1964 (he was shot and beaten to death by a frightened motel manager under questionable circumstances), Cooke relied heavily on his gospel roots to define the soul sound, pioneering much of the African-American music yet to come.

Sam Cooke (above—bottom row, second from right—and right) began his career as a gospel singer with the Soul Stirrers (above). The temptations of fame and fortune lured him into a career as a pop singer that was cut short by his murder in 1964.

Singer Fanny Lou Hamer was an unlikely hero of the Civil Rights movement. In word, deed, and song, this sharecropper's wife from Ruleville, Mississippi, was a tireless soldier in the battle for racial equality.

Gospel and the Civil Rights Movement

Gospel has often been the guiding light in the struggles of African Americans not just for survival and freedom, but for basic human rights. As the offshoot of the work song and the spiritual, gospel is a natural vehicle for the expression of perseverance in the face of adversity; it seems logical then that the gospel tradition was instrumental in the Civil Rights movement of the sixties. During this period songs from all kinds of grass-roots traditions—especially gospel standards—galvanized a community dedicated to effecting a fundamental change in the attitudes of Americans toward race and equality. Finally, though it may seem at first glance that the Civil Rights movement was at its core a political upheaval, it is instructive to remember that one of the greatest advocates for equal rights, and the movement's greatest martyr, was the Reverend Martin Luther King, Jr., a Baptist minister.

Another heroic figure from the same period was a sharecropper's wife by the name of Fanny Lou Hamer (1919–1977), a singer whose commitment both to equal rights and to the Christian religion made her an untiring civil rights activist. Her career as a political agitator began late in her life, in the summer of 1962. That year, the Student Non-Violent Coordinating Committee (SNCC) went to Ruleville, Mississippi, to organize a voting registration drive for blacks in a thoroughly Jim Crow community. Typically, the eighteen brave people who had boarded a bus for the courthouse in Indianola were denied their voting rights through an outrageous

technicality. The harrassment continued on their return journey: the bus was stopped by police on the grounds that it was the same color as a school bus. Fanny Lou Hamer's voice could be heard trailing from the back of the bus, singing hymns and spirituals, urging strength and patience.

In the following years, Fanny Lou Hamer survived through incredible hardships to express the healing power of love and the equality of all human beings in the eyes of the Creator through her gospel performances at rallies and demonstrations across the country. She was often harrassed, and sometimes brutalized (in an incident in Charleston, South Carolina, she was jailed and severely beaten by police, sustaining permanent and debilitating damage to her kidneys and left eye). Undaunted, she rose up after every occasion to fight for equal rights. She was quoted as saying "I've been sick and tired for so long that I'm sick and tired of being sick and tired," a sentiment that is etched on her tombstone in Ruleville, where she is buried on land purchased by the Freedom Farm Cooperative.

James Cleveland (1930–1991)

Perhaps the most influential gospel figure during the seventies was James Cleveland, who began organizing the Gospel Singers Workshop Convention in 1968, bringing in more singers and attendees than ever before. By 1970, through the innovative additions of choir workshops, seminars, classes, and other informational events, the convention had swollen to five thousand members, almost twice its size in 1968. For the first time, the needs of gospel choirs and their associates were being adequately addressed by the convention; services that were impossible to obtain in their local communities were now being made available to the poorer congregations.

James Cleveland was raised in Chicago, where he began his musical career as a pianist, playing behind the legendary Roberta Martin. Dinah Washington, who had once been the lead singer for

Opposite page: The 1963 March on Washington was a turning point in the Civil Rights struggle. Mahalia Jackson sang a spiritual as prelude to the Reverend Martin Luther King's now-famous "I Have a Dream" speech. Inset: Reverend King leads a 1968 march in Memphis flanked by Southern Christian Leadership Committee president, the Reverend Ralph Abernathy (right), and Bishop Julian Smith (left).

Called the "Crown Prince of Gospel," the Reverend James Cleveland wrote more than four hundred gospel songs and recorded over one hundred albums, sixteen of which were million-sellers. He helped Quincy Jones with the soundtrack for the historic miniseries Roots *and was the first gospel performer honored with a star on Hollywood's "Walk of Fame."*

Sallie Martin's group, was also a major influence on Cleveland, demonstrating to him that there was a marriage to be made between gospel and the more secular forms of African-American music, most notably the blues. His synthesis of the two forms electrified the gospel community in the mid-fifties and established him at the forefront of the new, hard gospel. During this period he worked with many gospel luminaries and with such ensembles as Albertina Walker's famous Caravans.

In the sixties, Cleveland teamed up with the Angelic Choir of Nutley, New Jersey, with whom he subsequently recorded many albums. His gruff, raw voice proved to be the perfect medium for conveying the intense emotional and religious content of his songs. In 1972, he and the Southern California Community Choir and Aretha Franklin recorded a double-album, *Amazing Grace*, in what amounted to a return to the style that had guided Franklin's early career. Touring on the evangelical circuit as a child, she had often performed in the same venues as Cleveland; it seemed only natural that they should team up again.

The Here and After

By the eighties, gospel was becoming more and more mainstream as artists began to merge the style with an increasing number of popular musical formats. Ironically, considering that he had been somewhat revolutionary in the fifties, James Cleveland rejected this popular movement. His reentrenchment along more conservative lines was illustrative of the general split that occurred during the eighties, dividing the gospel community into the traditional and contemporary factions.

The forties and fifties were arguably the peak period for the popularity of gospel, at least in its original manifestation. Once the world got hold of the music that had sprung from the aching spirit of slavery, changes were bound to occur. Gospel's rhythms and primal power were explosive fuel for subsequent musical styles, all of which owe the form a significant debt; soul, funk, disco, and even rap are all descended to some degree from the gospel tradition. This is not to say, however, that gospel has vanished; on the contrary, gospel today is an active and lucrative international industry, enjoying widespread popularity.

Contemporary gospel singers and choirs are acclaimed both inside and outside the gospel community, winning Dove Awards (gospel's top honor, bestowed by the Gospel Music Association) and Grammy Awards, and performing to sold-out crowds in town halls, stadiums, and concert halls throughout the country. Artists such as Shirley Caesar (1939–   ), who is considered one of the most accom-

The Reverend Milton Brunson & The Thompson Community Choir at a concert in 1991. Under Brunson's leadership, The Thompson Community Choir has been a fertile training ground for many talented young gospel singers.

plished gospel singers of the day, The Mighty Clouds of Joy, and Reverend Milton Brunson & The Thompson Community Singers continue to thrill audiences with their interpretations of the gospel idiom. These, not surprisingly, are only a few of the gospel artists popular today.

That its creators might not sanction the rampant commercialization that now surrounds the music is beside the point. The important and abiding truth is that gospel lives and is still practiced with the same fervor, in many of the same places, and to express the same sentiments: the glory of God, the salvation of humankind, and the enduring hope for peace and harmony in a troubled world.

Bibliography

Brooks, Tilford. *America's Black Musical Heritage.* Englewood Cliffs, N. J.: Prentice Hall, 1984.

Broughton, Viv. *Black Gospel: An Illustrated History of the Gospel Sound.* London: Blandford Press, 1985.

Fischer, Mark Miles. *Negro Slave Songs in the United States.* New York: Citadel Press, 1990.

Heilbut, Anthony. *The Gospel Sound.* New York: Anchor Press/Doubleday, 1985.

Reagon, Bernice Johnson, ed. *We'll Understand It Better By and By.* Washington, D.C.: Smithsonian Institution Press, 1992.

Recommended Reading

Blackwell, Lois S. *Wings of the Dove: The Story of Gospel Music in America.* Norfolk, W.Va.: Donning Publishers, 1978.

Courlander, Harold. *Negro Folk Music, USA.* New York: Columbia University Press, 1963.

Goreau, L. *Just Mahalia, Baby.* Gretna, Calif.: Pelican Publishing Co., Inc., 1975.

Harris, Michael W. *The Rise of Gospel Blues: The Music of Thomas Dorsey in the Urban Church.* New York: Oxford University Press, 1992.

Haydon, Geoffrey, and Dennis Marks. *Repercussions: A Celebration of African American Music.* London: Century Publishers, 1985.

Jackson, Jesse. *Make a Joyful Noise Unto the Lord!* Boston: G.K. Hall & Co., 1974.

Jackson, Mahalia, and Evan Wylie. *Movin' On Up.* London: Hawthorne Books, 1966.

Jones, Ralph H. *Charles Albert Tindley: Prince of Preachers.* Nashville: Abingdon Press, 1982.

Maultsby, Portia K. *Afro-American Religious Music: A Study in Musical Diversity.* New York: Wittenberg University, 1986.

Robeson, Paul. *Here I Stand.* Boston: Beacon Press, 1971.

Southern, Eileen. *The Music of Black Americans: A History.* New York: W.W. Norton, 1982.

Recommended Listening

Fairfield Four, The. *One World, One People, One God, One Religion.* Nashboro.

_____. *Standing In The Safety Zone.* Warner/Alliance.

Franklin, Aretha. *The Gospel Sound of Aretha Franklin.* Atlantic.

Green, Al. *Soul Survivor.* A&M.

Griffin, Gloria. *I'm So Grateful.* Savoy.

Heavenly Gospel Singers. *Heavenly Gospel Singers.* Heritage.

Jackson, Mahalia. *Gospels, Spirituals & Hymns.* Sony.

_____. *Mahalia Jackson's Greatest Hits.* Columbia/Sony.

Original Five Blind Boys of Mississippi. *Uncloudy Day/Will the Circle Be Unbroken.* Veejay.

Pilgrim Travelers. *The Best of the Pilgrim Travelers.* Vols. I and II. Specialty.

Soul Stirrers. *The Soul Stirrers Featuring Sam Cooke.* Specialty.

Sweet Honey in the Rock. *Feeling Something Drawing Me On.* Flying Fish.

Tharpe, Sister Rosetta. *The One and Only Sister Rosetta Tharpe:Precious Memories.* Savoy.

Various. *Jubilation! Great Gospel Performances.* Vol 1: *Black Gospel.* Mahalia Jackson, Aretha Franklin, the Edwin Hawkins Singers, et al. Vol 2: *More Black Gospel.* The Staple Singers, the Rev. James Cleveland, the Soul Stirrers with Sam Cooke, et al. Vol 3: *Country Gospel.* The Carter Family, Hank Williams, Kitty Wells, Patsy Cline, Ricky Skaggs, et al. Rhino.

Ward, Clara. *The Best of the Ward Singers of Philadelphia, Pa.* Savoy.

Photography Credits

Cover collage–clockwise from top left:
©Tim Gibson/Envision; ©Dennis Hallinan/FPG International; ©Terry Wild Studios; Globe Photos; ©David Redferns/Retna Ltd.; ©Courtesy Estate of Morton Roberts.

AP/Wide World Photos: pp. 65, 66. ©Archive Photos: pp. 11, 20 top, 25 top. ©Ray Avery's Jazz Archives: p. 35. Frank Driggs Collection: pp. 10 bottom, 34, 50, 55 left, 59 bottom, 64 top. Courtesy of Sherry Sherrod DuPree Archives: pp. 30, 53. Courtesy Fisk University Library: p. 24. FPG International: p. 22. Globe Photos: pp. 6, 60. Courtesy of Hampton University Archives: pp. 27, 28–29, 29 right. Courtesy of William Ransom Hogan Jazz Archive, Tulane University: pp. 38, 39, 40–41, 45 , 46. Ron Keith/©Warner Bros. Records: p. 59 top. ©Ross Marino/Retna Ltd.: p. 10 top. National Museum of American Art, Washington, DC/Art Resource, NY: p. 14 top. North Wind Picture Archives: pp. 12, 13, 15, 16, 17, 20 bottom, 21. Michael Ochs Archives: pp. 33, 48 , 55 right, 56–57, 57 top, 58, 62 right, 64 bottom. Neal Peters Collection/Frank Teti: p. 51. Neal Peters Collection: p. 54. ©David Redfern/ Retna Ltd.: pp. 2–3, 62 top left & bottom, 68. © Courtesy of Estate of Morton Roberts: p. 37. Scala/Art Resource, NY: pp. 18–19. © Stock Montage, Inc., Chicago, IL: pp. 14 bottom, 25 bottom, 26. © Bruce W.Talamon/Michael Ochs Archives/ Venice, CA: p. 9. ©Ernest C. Withers, Sr.: p. 42. Courtesy of Word/Epic Records: p. 69.

Index